NORTH AMERICAN INDIAN
SURVIVAL SKILLS

NORTH AMERICAN INDIAN SURVIVAL SKILLS

KAREN LIPTAK

FRANKLIN WATTS
NEW YORK/LONDON/TORONTO/SIDNEY
A FIRST BOOK/1990

Illustrations by Vantage Art

Cover photograph courtesy of: American Museum of Natural History

Photographs courtesy of: American Museum of Natural History: pp. 8, 12, 35,
36, 39 bottom, 41, 55; Karen Liptak: p. 11; New York Public Library, Picture
Collection: pp. 15, 24, 32 bottom, 42, 48 bottom; Historical Picture
Service: p. 19; Photo Researchers: pp. 21 (Jim W. Grace), 32 top
(Francois Gohier), 48 top (Jill Durrance), 51 bottom (Tom McHugh/Indian
City, USA); Hudson's Bay Company Archives/Provincial Archives of Manitoba:
pp. 23, 57; Gamma-Liaison: p. 27 (Eric Bouvet); The University Museum/University
of Pennsylvania: p. 28; Jeff Greenberg Agency: pp. 39 top, 51 top (both
Betty Groskin), 60 (Saul Mayer).

Library of Congress Cataloging in Publication Data

Liptak, Karen.
    North American Indian survival skills / Karen Liptak.
        p.   cm. — (A First book)
    Includes bibliographical references.
    Summary: Describes methods used by various North American
tribes to find food, shelter, clothing, and medicines.
    ISBN 0-531-10870-8
    1. Indians of North America—Social life and customs—Juvenile
literature. 2. Wilderness survival—North America—Juvenile
literature. [1. Indians of North America—Social life and customs.
2. Wilderness survival. 3. Survival.] I. Title. II. Series.
E98.S7L57   1990
613.6′9′08997—dc20   90-12354 CIP AC

First Paperback Edition 1992
0-531-15642-7

CONTENTS

With grateful thanks to Willy Whitefeather,
who introduced me to the spirit of
the North American Indians.

North American Indians are currently called
American Indians, as well as Native Americans.
However, at a recent Reno, Nevada, Indian powwow,
most Indians who were surveyed said that they
preferred being known as American Indians.

Using the resources of the earth, early
North American Indians built shelters,
found food, and made clothing.

THE INDIAN WAY

Today, we all live very different lives from those of the early inhabitants of North America. We buy our food in supermarkets and our clothes in department or specialty stores. We use cars to get around, and when the family car breaks down, we take it to a garage mechanic to repair it.

The early North American Indians had none of these resources. Instead, they relied upon Mother Earth in ways that are unfamiliar to most of us. The Indians were good at many skills that helped them survive in the days before supermarkets, department and specialty stores, cars, and garages existed. They could build shelters, hunt, skin, and tan animal hides or skins, gather plants, create tools and weapons, and make natural threads. With the raw materials they found around them, the Indians created a life-style that was both efficient and successful. Survival thinking was second nature to them.

The Indians' ingenuity helped them stay alive in a variety of regions, from desert to tundra, woodland to plains, coastal areas to prairie. Yet, no matter where they lived, the Indians treated Mother Earth with great respect.

Willy Whitefeather, who is of Cherokee descent, gives talks and workshops on outdoor survival skills at schools around the United States. He shares the lessons that his Indian ancestors taught him with today's young people. And wherever he goes, Willy reminds boys and girls to give thanks for whatever they take from Mother Earth.

As he says, "That is the Indian way."

SURVIVAL SHELTERS

Shelter was one of the major needs of the North American Indians. Their dwellings were made from many materials, including trees and plants, as well as stones, mud, clay, and animal hides.

Where food was abundant, the people of some tribes built permanent shelters. In other areas, they lived by following the herds that they hunted. For these people, portable shelters were essential.

Willy Whitefeather introduces a school group in Tucson, Arizona, to survival techniques.

Tipis of poles and buffalo hide provided summer homes.

The *tipi* of the Plains Indians is the most well-known portable home. A tipi was made from poles (often made from pine), a covering of buffalo skins, and sinew. Sinew is animal tendon, the long fibers that join muscle to bone. Sinew was used as a thread to sew the animal skins together.

A pointed tool called an *awl* was needed to build a tipi. Awls were often made from buffalo bone; they were used to punch holes in the animal hide. Another tool made from bone that was used in making tipis was the needle.

Building a tipi was a woman's work. The woman making the tipi prepared a feast, which she invited other women to share. Those who accepted her invitation were expected to also help her construct the tipi.

After the meal, prayers were said. Then the women got to work. Three or four poles that had been stripped, trimmed, and dried in the sun were lashed together a few feet from the top. Then the poles were raised and spread out at the base.

Some tribes traditionally added more poles; the more poles used, the tighter the buffalo skin covering could be stretched around the tipi.

The covering was sewn together with sinew, then tied, inside out, to a long pole. The pole and cover were lifted high. A hole was left on the top, so that smoke from fires built inside the tipi could escape.

Although tipis weren't hard to make, their construction took some time. But many North American Indians had shelters that were easier to produce.

One of the simplest homes was the *wikiup*. A wikiup required about twenty wooden sticks with natural forks in them. The sticks were placed so that they all leaned toward each other.

The Paiute Indians of the Great Basin topped their wikiups with boughs of the Sierra juniper tree. These they wove into place. Other coverings included bark, grass, and reeds.

But what if a traveler needed a home in an emergency and lacked even the few hours it took to build a wikiup? A fallen tree surrounded with some additional branches could provide a quick refuge. The favorite natural protection of the American Indians in the West was a shallow cave or rock shelter.

PUTTING THINGS TOGETHER

Cordage—A Survival Necessity

The North American Indians considered cordage to be as great a necessity as shelter, food, and clothing. Cordage includes fasteners such as rope, twine, cord, string, and line. These were used for everything from dwellings and nets to bows, traps, and clothing.

Cordage can be made from a variety of animal materials. The most common animal cordage in North

Cordage was used in making shelters, clothes,
and more; here, in a George Catlin painting,
a Plains warrior uses it to rope a wild pony.

America came from the sinew of moose, deer, elk, and
buffalo. Sinew is very strong and has a natural "glue."

Parts of many plants are also made into cordage.
Among these are the bark of slippery elm, moose-
wood, and red cedar. In the Southwest, the leaves of
the yucca provide fiber, as do those of the agave
plant. Grasses can be used, too, as well as milkweed,
fiber, sagebrush, and wild hemp.

Some plant fibers were stripped away easily from
the plant without any additional work. Other fibers

were gathered by pounding the part of the plant to be used with a stone until the fibers began to separate. The fibers were placed in a container of water since they were easier to work with when wet.

There were a few common methods for making cordage. Here is one as described by Willy White-feather:

1. Take four strands of fiber. Twist two strands together between your thumb and forefinger (A). Then twist the other two strands together (B).

2. Lay the first two-strand twist (A) over the second two-strand twist. Now twist all four strands of fiber together.

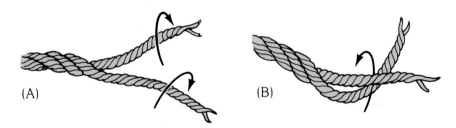

(A)   (B)

3. Repeat steps 1 and 2 again and again.

4. Lengthen your cordage by carefully placing two new strands of fiber next to the last 2–4 inches (5–10 cm) of (A) and (B) and start twisting all four strands together. Repeat, adding two new strands each time, until the cordage is long enough.

The finished cord could be created on the spot, or carried along on trips.

Glue, Too

The North American Indians also knew how to make glue, which was used to seal objects such as baskets and canoes.

In the days before Krazy Glue, the Indians made their glues from deer and buffalo hides, hooves, and horn. The skin, oil, and internal organs of fish were also turned into glue. So, too, was the gum or sap of pine, black spruce, and chokecherry trees.

After most glues were collected, they had to be heated, and then cooled and stored in a hardened form. Later, when the glues were needed, they were softened by reheating. Because glues required storage and processing before use, they were more difficult to transport than cordage. Therefore, cordage was used more often than glue.

HUNTING

Hunting was an important part of life in the North American Indian tribes. The people ate animal meat, and among many tribes, animal hides were used to make clothing and shelters. The Indians made tools and weapons from animal bones, and blankets from animal hair. Much of their lives revolved around the pursuit of animals, both large and small.

The North American Indians survived by learning how to read Mother Earth like a book, to know which animals made which footprints.

Hunters could also figure out when footprints were made, and how fast the animal was moving. They found clues to an animal's whereabouts in still other ways. Animal droppings provided valuable information. Were they warm and moist? Then the animal may have been there not too long before.

Plants told stories, too. Neatly clipped vegetation was a sign that rabbits had passed by recently, whereas coarsely ripped plants suggested that a deer might have just eaten. A barren berry patch? A sign that a bear might be near.

The Indians came to know the life-style of the animals they stalked: what they ate, how they traveled, where they slept. Their wealth of knowledge enabled Indian hunters to use their time wisely, and only to go after the likeliest prey.

Hunting techniques varied depending upon the animal sought. For most large animals, stalking and ambushes of various types were used. Community hunts might drive herds of animals toward a V shape of logs, poles, brush, or stones where hunters waited for them with weapons.

Hunters also acted alone. A solitary Eastern Woodlands hunter might eat nothing but bracken shoots for a few days, so that his human odor was less likely to frighten away deer. Elsewhere, hunters rubbed themselves with plants known to attract deer.

Indian hunters also used disguises. Some deer hunters made costumes from the skin of a deer's head and neck. The Navajo even attached strips of deerskin to the headpiece, which they pulled to make the deer head's ears wiggle.

Disguised as buffalo, Indian hunters close in on their prey.

In the Southwest and the Eastern Woodlands, one way to catch deer was to light a ring of fire on the grass around them. This frightened the deer, causing them to huddle in the center of the circle. They became easy prey for the hunters.

Although such methods may seem cruel to us, remember that most North American Indians didn't hunt animals for sport. And the Indians always gave thanks for the animals they caught and relied upon for so much.

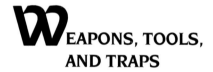

WEAPONS, TOOLS, AND TRAPS

Many kinds of weapons and tools were used by North American Indians. Some of the simplest of these were made from stone. Stone flaking is the oldest stone-working technique. It involves chipping a narrow razor-sharp piece of stone, called a *flake*, from a larger stone, known as a *core*.

Flakes were used for cutting or scraping animal skin. Some were further worked on to form an arrowhead or a spear point.

Bone was also useful for making tools and weap-

Arrowheads, such as this Apache sample found
in west Texas, were worked from stone flakes.

ons on the trail. Since bone is not as hard as stone,
great care had to be taken when working with it. However, as bone ages it hardens and becomes easier to
work with. The shinbones of deer were used to make
good awls and needles.

Traps are devices for capturing animals that can
work even when the hunter isn't there. Traps were set
primarily along paths with many plants and heavy an-

imal traffic. The plants kept animals from spotting the traps. The two basic traps were the snare and the deadfall.

A snare consists of a noose with a knot that is often attached to a triggering device. Material for snares could be hair and plant fiber, sinew, or rawhide. Small snares could be set to catch birds or small animals. Larger snares were used to catch deer, caribou, moose, and bear.

Deadfalls were as effective as snares. These devices used a heavy object to kill the animal. One of the simplest Indian deadfalls was the figure-four deadfall. Two sticks of equal length were trimmed and sharpened at one end. One stick was placed in the ground. The other was notched and placed horizontally across it. A third and longer stick was cut, notched, and positioned to form the third side of a triangle. Now you had a figure that looked like the number 4.

A heavy log or stone was then supported by the third stick. Food was placed on the horizontal stick as bait. When an animal went for the bait, its movement caused the delicately balanced sticks to fall, and the log or stone to tumble down and crush it.

When food was very scarce, traps were checked often. Otherwise, as Willy Whitefeather says, "A good trapper of conscience checks traps at least once daily, so that animals needn't suffer for a long time."

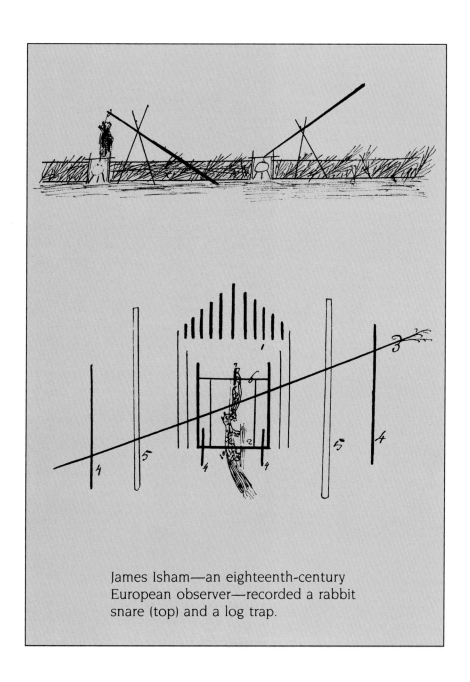

James Isham—an eighteenth-century
European observer—recorded a rabbit
snare (top) and a log trap.

Bow and Arrows

The bow and arrow was the favorite weapon of most North American Indians. Bows were made out of young trees, called *saplings*. Superior bow woods included yew, osage orange, ash, and chokeberry.

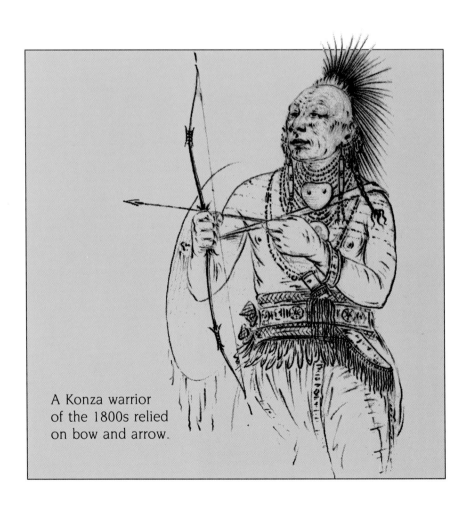

A Konza warrior of the 1800s relied on bow and arrow.

The material used most often for bowstrings was deer or moose sinew. Since sinew stretches in wet weather, Indians in damp areas often made their bowstrings from strong plant fibers instead.

Arrow shafts were made from reeds, canes, or stems of almost any wood. Feathers were often attached to the shafts. These made the arrow's flight more accurate. Arrow shafts were tipped with points made from bone, antler, or stone.

In many tribes, arrows were carried in a stiff case known as a *quiver*. The Ojibwa of the Great Lakes region made their quivers from buckskin.

Indians of the forest made short arrows, since these were less likely to get snagged on branches and bushes. Elsewhere in North America, long arrows were preferred.

Willy Whitefeather offers this suggestion: "If a bow is needed quickly for small game, I would look around for any tree with a curved branch in it about 3 feet (1 m) long. I'd cut it and shape and notch the ends, then make a string and some arrows. However, I'd just sharpen the points of the arrows with a stone or knife—instead of taking the time to make arrowheads.

"If I didn't have any feathers, I'd cut three leaves so that they were straight, instead of round at the top. Then I would slit the arrow shaft and insert the three trimmed leaves into it so that their center spines lined up with the shaft.

"This simple bow and arrows would get me a rabbit or raccoon for dinner, or by cutting notches in the arrow and fastening a line to it, I could shoot a fish and pull it in and eat."

FISHING

From one generation to another, North American Indians passed on the secrets of the water just as they passed on the secrets of the land. They knew where and when the fish were biting, as well as many techniques for catching them.

Some fish could be grasped by Indians who felt with their bare hands among the crevices along streams. On the Atlantic and Pacific coasts, shellfish such as mussels and oysters were also picked up by hand.

Elsewhere, some fish could be taken by dazing them with plants containing poison. In California, the crushed root of the soap plant was dropped into a still body of water, such as a pool. The poison in the root stunned the fish, which then floated to the surface.

Fish were a major food source for some subarctic
tribes, and for the Eskimo of Alaska.

Spearing Salmon, as photographed by Edward S. Curtis (1868–1952), a photographer of Indian life.

According to reports, the fish caught in this way remained edible, although poisoned.

Spearfishing was a technique used by some North American Indians. Spears were made from wood as well as from bone. Some spears were pronged and used with a stabbing action. Other spears were barbed and thrown. Some barbed spears had semidetachable heads that were attached with thread to the spear. These heads were most easily made from small deer antlers.

Indians also caught fish with nets. The Eastern Woodlands tribes made their nets from plant fibers. On the Plains, animal hides and sinew were used, whereas along the Northwest Coast nets were made from the inner bark of trees.

The most common Indian fishing gear was simple to make, and consisted of a hook and line suspended from a pole.

One of the easiest hooks to make was the skewer, or gorge hook ("gorge" refers to the throat). For this you need a hardwood twig that is naturally pointed on both ends. Or, you can whittle a point on each end with a sharp stone or a knife. Hardwoods include hickory, oak, beech, locust, and birch. A sharp sliver of bone can also make a good skewer hook.

Gorge hook

A fishing pole for this hook can be made from the trunk of a sapling no more than 5 feet (1½ m) long.

Fishing line is tied to the pole. Some excellent fibers for line are made from stinging nettle, milkweed, and dogbane. The hook is tied to the line, then covered with bait to attract the fish. Worms, crickets, grasshoppers, and minnows all make good bait.

When a fish swallows the bait, the entire skewer hook catches inside its mouth or in its stomach. In either case, the fish is trapped.

Indians cleaned their fish as soon as possible after catching them, because the guts of a fish spoil its taste if they are left in too long. Removing the guts also reduced the weight of the fish and made them easier to carry home to the main village. Some fish were eaten fresh, whereas others were dried or smoked to preserve them for future meals.

PLANTS ALONG THE PATH

Although meat and fish were basic foods for most North American Indians, over fifteen hundred different plants were eaten by them. Throughout the land, knowing which plants to pick and when to pick them as well as how to preserve them were valuable survival skills. As with animals, no edible or otherwise usable part of a plant went to waste.

The following are some of the plants Indians ate and used along the trails across North America:

Acorns. In California acorns were the principal plant food. They were also important in the Eastern Woodlands. Acorns were roasted, boiled, or crushed into flour to make bread. They could also be made into mush. However, most acorns had a bitter taste and had to be treated with many washings before they tasted good enough to eat.

Agave. Also known as the century plant or mescal, this was one of the major foods of the southwestern American Indians. Although the juice of the leaves of the raw plant can cause a serious irritation, the center stalk was edible when it was cooked. The crown, the flowers, and seeds were also eaten. The juice from the cooked crowns could be made into a liquor, whereas the liquid from the agave flowers could become a sweet, nonalcoholic drink.

Arrowhead. This plant was a major food in some parts of the Eastern Woodlands, where its underground stem was made into flour, as well as eaten like a potato.

In Arizona, Papago Indians harvest fruits from the saguaro plant.

Ojibwa and other North American Indians in the Great Lakes region harvested wild rice by canoe.

Camas. A member of the lily family, the camas was the major plant food on the Plateau and the western Plains. The bulbs were harvested in the summer when they were in bloom and could be easily told apart from a similar, but poisonous plant known as the death camas. The bulbs were roasted and dried, then stored for the winter.

Cattails. This plant, with its sausage-shaped head, was most popular as a food in the Great Basin, California, and the Southwest. A true survival plant, parts of cattails were used to make mats, baskets, capes, and cradles. Dressings for wounds and "diapers" were made from cattail fluff.

When used for food, the plants' thick roots were cooked. The shoots were also edible, either raw or cooked. In some areas, the pollen produced by the flowering head of the cattail was made into bread or mush. When boiled, the green head could be eaten like corn on the cob.

Ferns. Ferns were used mainly by the Indians of British Columbia, who lived in the wet forests where they grew. Favored parts were the fronds (large, young leaves). The fronds of some ferns were known as *fiddleheads*, because they resemble a fiddle's neck. In the spring, fiddleheads are thick and juicy.

Greenbrier. The roots of these thorny vines were the major wild plant in the Southeast. They were chopped for use in making bread or soup. The shoots and fruit of the greenbrier were also edible.

Indian Breadroot or Prairie Turnip. This was an important food, especially on the Plains. The Indians there peeled the roots and ate them raw. The roots were also boiled, or roasted, or ground into flour for soup or bread. They could be dried for future use.

Maple Syrup. The sap of nearly a dozen different North American maple trees was collected by the Indians of the Great Lakes region. Sap is a sugary liquid that flows through plant tissues. The Indians gathered it in containers made from tree trunks. Sap was boiled down and strained to form syrup. Some syrup was made into sugar and sprinkled over food.

Mesquite. This was one of the major foods of the southwestern United States. The ripe beans of the mesquite were ground into meal, which was mixed with water to form cakes. The cakes were dried and eaten raw or cooked. Ripe beans could also be dried.

Wild Fruit. North America was filled with luscious fruits of all kinds, including blueberries, raspberries, and strawberries. Currants, rose hips, grapes, and plums were also eaten by most Indians.

When gathering berries, many American Indians raked the bushes with their fingers. Others placed blankets on the ground to catch the berries, and then beat the bushes with sticks. Berries were eaten immediately as well as dried.

In the woodlands, sap was collected from maple
trees to be boiled down into syrup.

Digging sticks were used to break up the soil, make holes for planting seeds, and dig out roots.

Digging Stick

Edible plant roots were easy to find. However, most grow deep and digging them out was not so easy. Much time and effort was saved with a simple device called a *digging stick*. This was a hardwood stick about 3 feet (1 m) long, stripped of all bark and with its point sharpened. Digging sticks enabled Indians to pry and lift roots to the surface with more leverage than if they used only their hands.

Poison Oak, Ivy, Sumac, and Others

The American Indians were well acquainted with poison oak, ivy, and sumac. They treated each with caution as well as respect. Whenever they neared one of these plants they called the plant "my friend" to keep it from getting angry and harming them.

Poison sumac is not as common as poison ivy or poison oak. However, it contains much more poison. Drawings of the three troublesome plants are shown to help you identify them.

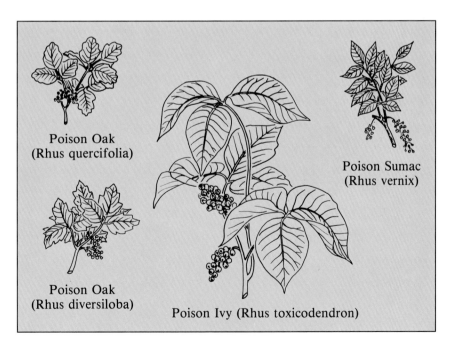

Poison Oak
(Rhus quercifolia)

Poison Oak
(Rhus diversiloba)

Poison Sumac
(Rhus vernix)

Poison Ivy (Rhus toxicodendron)

Some poisonous plants are relatively easy to identify; others are not. For instance, dogbane is a deadly plant that looks like milkweed—parts of which can be eaten if cooked. The edible wild carrot can be mistaken for its deadly look-alike, water hemlock. As mentioned earlier, when camas is not in bloom, it can be mistaken for death camas, a deadly plant.

It is always advisable to ask an expert's advice before eating any plant that is strange to you. Indian boys and girls spend many years being instructed by their elders to prevent them from making mistakes that could kill them.

PREPARING WILDERNESS FOOD

Indians in western North America cooked roots and greens as well as meat and other food in a steaming pit. They dug a pit in the ground, lined it with stones, and then built a fire in it. After an hour, the coals were scraped out and a layer of wet grass was placed over the stones. The food was set on the grass and covered with more wet grass. Water was poured on the food. When the water reached the hot stones, steam

North American Indians used various methods of roasting, steam cooking, and pit cooking to prepare foods.

formed. Then the pit was quickly covered with flat rocks or a piece of hide. Finally, dirt was heaped over the entire pit to seal in the steam. The food cooked in such a pit for several hours.

In other regions of the country, food was often roasted directly in the flames or wrapped and baked in the ashes of a fire.

Another widespread heating technique also relied upon the use of hot stones. First, a pit was dug and lined with leaves. Nearby, a pile of stones was heated. Then the stones were lifted up with two forked sticks and dropped into the pit. Over these hot stones you could roast small animals, or plants. If you lined the pit with animal hide or stones and filled it with water, you could boil your supper instead.

Dried seeds, roots, and berries were stored in pits at the backs of rock shelters. Such pits kept the food dry and helped Indians survive during lean seasons.

Preserving Meat

The prehistoric hunters of the High Plains preserved meat by drying it. They cut the meat into long, thin strips, which they left out in the sun. Such dried meat is known as *jerky*.

Jerky can be eaten as is, or cooked in stews. It was also turned into pemmican, which served the same

To prepare pemmican, one person hangs strips of meat
on a drying rack; another pounds meat with a hammer.

purpose as the "trail mix" that campers take along
today. Pemmican was a mixture of dried meat, fat,
and dried berries, rolled into small balls and smeared
with deer's blood. The blood formed a crust that kept
flies from getting at the meat.

Indians often carried pemmican along on trips,
since it kept much longer than jerky. They stored the
balls in waterproof bags, such as rawhide containers.

BUILDING A FIRE

Fires were a necessity almost everywhere. They were used for warmth and cooking, as well as for signaling, keeping away insects, and socializing. A blazing fire was a welcome sight to come home to.

This scene in a Mandan lodge shows community life centered around the fire.

Fires were built inside shelters, as well as out-doors.

The early North American Indians had to start their fires with only raw materials.

When Willy Whitefeather speaks at schools, he brings along an Indian "fire set" like the ones his ancestors used. This is a basic fire-starting apparatus. Tinder is material that burns easily. Shredded bark was one common tinder used by the North American Indians. They rubbed shreds of it between their hands to form a fluffy ball.

The bow-drill fire set was popular among Indians living in the northern part of the United States and Canada. It consists of four main parts, the fireboard (or hearth), the drill, the hand socket, and the bow.

The fireboard was often made from such woods as cedar, pine, poplar, and willow. In the Southwest, mesquite and yucca were used. The fireboard is a piece of wood with a notch cut in close to the edge.

The drill is made from the same wood as the fireboard. Its edges are rounded, and one end is sharpened, so that it looks like a thick pencil.

The hand socket is made from a block of hard wood. It protects the hand from the drill and helps the drill bore through the wood.

Excellent bows for bow-drill sets are made from a hickory or juniper branch with a natural bend to them.

The bark is peeled and notched on both ends. Then a rawhide or fiber cord is attached to each end of the bow. The cord fits loosely at first, but becomes tighter as you follow these directions.

Bow fire set

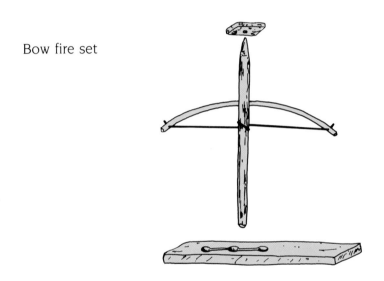

Here are the steps to make a fire with a fire drill. (NOTE: Never try to start a fire without an experienced fire-starter by your side.)

1. Place a handful of tinder, in the shape of a bird's nest, under the fireboard.

2. Rest the fireboard on the ground in front of you. Anchor it by putting your left foot on it. (If you are left-handed, reverse all instructions.) Kneel on your right knee. Place the socket in your left hand and

the bow in your right hand. Twirl the bowstring once around the drill, fit the socket above it, and position the bottom of the drill in the notch on the fireboard. Hold the drill steady by bracing your left arm around your left knee.

3. Slowly revolve the drill, with long, even motions, drawing the bow back and forth. (The cord becomes tighter as you work.) Gradually pick up your speed and press down harder on the socket. If you are successful, smoke will eventually appear. The smoke tells you that by your sawing action you are creating a hot coal in the fireboard's notch.

The coal comes from the fine sawdust shavings that you are forming. As you revolve the drill, those fine shavings clump together into the coal.

When the smoke gets heavy, drop the bow and drill, and lightly tap the fireboard. This loosens the red-hot coal so that it falls on the tinder. You can also use a small twig to drop the red-hot coal into the tinder. In either case, be careful not to lose the coal.

4. Slowly pick up the tinder, tightly pressing it around the hot coal. Hold the tinder high enough to keep the smoke out of your eyes, and breathe in and blow out gently. As you keep this up, the coal joins together even more to become tighter and harder. Soon the tinder glows and bursts into flame. The wind can help you if it blows on your back.

The North American Indians took their new fire to a fireplace, which was built within a ring of heavy stones to keep the fire from spreading. In the woods, campfires were set up away from anything that could easily burn, such as rotten logs, dry grass, and low-hanging tree limbs.

Kindling was placed inside the fireplace. Kindling is small sticks of wood about the size of wooden matches. This is the wood that keeps the fire going. The hot coal was transferred from the tinder to the kindling wood. Then the kindling ignited the logs above it, which are the fuel to keep the fire burning.

During Willy's talks, he tells that when Indians were lost in the woods, they knew to set up camp while it was still light enough to see what they were doing. Then they built two fires, one in front of them and the other behind them. That way they didn't have to keep turning around to stay warm.

For the back fire, the Indians dug down two inches deep and made the fire in a pit that was as wide as they were and as long as their backs from head to buttocks. When they were ready to go to sleep, they put out the fire and spread out the red-hot coals in it with a stick. Then, with their hands, they poured 2 inches (5 cm) of dirt over the coals, being careful to cover all the coals and pat down the earth well. Now they could lie down. The heat would come up through the dirt and keep them warm all night.

CONTAINERS

Containers were important survival devices. They were needed for gathering, storing, and cooking food. Some North American Indians made pottery containers. Others were made from stone, rawhide, and plant materials.

Woven baskets were used in many regions. People on the Northwest Coast wove their baskets from the inner bark of cedar. On the Plateau, baskets were woven from cedar, spruce, and juniper, as well as rush and cattail. Many southeastern tribes wove baskets from the stems of cane.

In California, baskets were woven out of pine roots, as well as willow and hazel twigs. In the Southwest, cottonwood and mulberry were used to make baskets. The materials for most woven baskets were first dried completely after they were gathered. Then the materials were soaked and kept moist while the baskets were being woven.

Birch bark was used throughout North America because many kinds of containers could be made from it as soon as the bark was peeled from trees.

Birch bark didn't have to be woven. It could be shaped in a variety of forms. The edges were punched with an awl and sewn together with fibers from the

In Oklahoma,
a member of the
Choctaw tribe
prepares material
for weaving
a basket.

Pottery containers
were often used
to collect and
carry water.

root of the spruce tree. Containers could be made waterproof by coating the outside seams with pitch, a sticky substance from the sap of trees such as pine.

FINDING WATER

Water is vital for human survival, and the North American Indians knew about many hidden places where it could be found. They searched near the tops of mountains and the bases of trees. They located water beneath the surface of damp and muddy ground, as well as near lush vegetation and animal trails.

In some regions, the Indians collected water by mopping up the morning dew from rocks and plants. Today a handkerchief or shirt is the easiest mop to use. Otherwise, a fistful of dry grass will work, just as it has for centuries. Once mopped up, dew can be wrung into a container and saved.

In the desert, water is hard to find, yet it is available. Cacti contain water. The Southwest Indians sometimes carried with them chunks cut from the heart of the barrel cactus to suck on when they were thirsty.

The desert also contains "marker plants" that

grow where water is present. These include cottonwoods, cattails, hackberries, and willows.

During the winter, clean white snow was eaten by thirsty travelers, who knew not to eat too much of it at one time so as not to become sick. At sea, where salt water cannot substitute for fresh water, Indians found water within fish.

Today we can carry along water-purification tablets to remove germs from water. In early times, all the water was pure. Later, Indians purified their water by boiling it.

SURVIVAL WARDROBES

In most parts of North America clothing was made from tanned animal hides. In the Southwest, it was also made from cotton that was woven on a loom, and on the Northwest Coast, most clothing was made from cedar bark.

North American Indians knew how to skin animals, as well as how to soften, stretch, and tan their hides. They also used natural threads to lace together their fashions.

Untanned animal hide is known as *rawhide*. It was

In the Southwest, men and women often wore clothing woven on looms.

A buffalo hide is stretched out on a frame to dry.

used to make bags, ropes, containers, and more. Making good rawhide took several steps.

An animal was usually skinned soon after it was killed, since removing the skin was easiest at that time. Then the hide was soaked in water until the hair began to loosen. Next, the hide was laid out flat and the flesh side was scraped of all fat and excess tissue. A tool called a *flesher*, made from the long bone of a large animal, was often used for this chore.

After scraping, the hide was washed and cleaned, and then dried in the sun. Next, it was turned over, laid down flat again, and all the hair was removed with a hair scraper, another bone tool. Finally, the hide was pounded with a blunt stone hammer.

Skins that were intended for use in making clothing were generally tanned. This process took place after the hair was scraped off. The hide was thoroughly rubbed with a paste made from animal fat mixed with animal brains. Then the hide was washed. Often the final step was smoking the tanned hide.

Sandals and Moccasins

In the Southwest, Indians made sandals from plant material or hide. Yucca and other fibers were hand-woven and held onto the foot with cords.

However, the most common Indian footwear in North America was the moccasin. There were two main types, soft soled and hard soled.

In forest areas, soft-soled moccasins were preferred. But in the Plains and the Southwest, where the ground was more rocky, hard-soled moccasins were used.

Most moccasins were made from tanned deerskin sewn with sinew. Other threads came from plant fibers.

The tools needed were usually a knife or sharpened stone to cut the hide and an awl to punch holes for the thread.

For wintertime moccasins, the hair on the hide might be left on and this side became the cozy inside of the moccasin. For warmer seasons, the hair was scraped from the hide and the hair side became the outside of the moccasin.

When the weather was cold, padding was put inside the moccasins. Padding could be made from animal skins or dried grass. In wet weather, Indians took off their moccasins and went barefoot since the shoes could fall apart from moisture.

Indians on the trail usually had extra pairs of moccasins, since these shoes often didn't last very long.

Moving over the Land

Transporting Supplies

Some of the American Indian tribes living on the Plains got most of their food and clothing from the buffalo. When the buffalo moved, the families of the tribe moved, too. Their survival greatly depended upon their ability to keep up with the herd.

The Indians dismantled their tipis and put all their belongings on a device known as a *travois*. This was like a sled made from two tipi poles. The poles were crossed in front of an animal's head, usually a horse or a dog. The other ends of the poles dragged on the ground. Halfway up the poles, rawhide strips were looped across the poles to form a loose net. The family's possessions were carried in this net.

Crossing Water

In some areas, travel by water was easier than travel by land. On the rivers and oceans of the Arctic, kayaks were used. A kayak had a wooden frame over which a covering of caribou skin or sealskin was stretched. A

The travois was used to carry belongings
when the families of a tribe moved.

hole was left in the center of the covering. This was called the cockpit, and the kayak's paddler sat in it.

Throughout the subarctic and in sections of the Eastern Woodlands, canoes provided the main transportation. These light, durable vessels usually had birch-bark covers and white cedar or spruce wood frames. They were held together by spruce roots.

Along the Northwest Coast, canoes were carved from solid logs of cedar. These dugouts were made by cutting down a tree and alternately burning and chopping the wood until it was trimmed to the proper shape.

Traveling Safely in Winter

Survival depended on knowing how to travel safely both day and night, throughout the year.

Snowshoes were a necessity during winters in the northern forests. The simplest snowshoes made by the North American Indians were known as *bearpaws*. To make a pair, straight branches were stripped and then bent into shape after being softened in boiling water or in steam.

Netting made from animal hide or bark was wrapped around the frame. A single piece of rope doubled and knotted twice around the foot and ankle served as a binding.

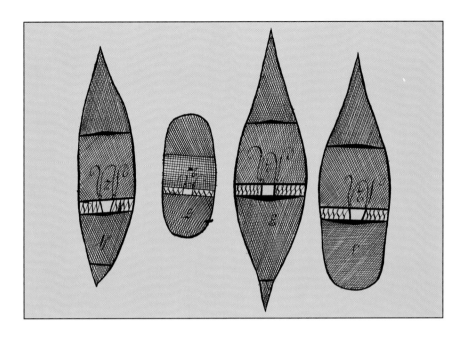

James Isham drew the various snowshoes used
in the Hudson Bay region about 1740.

Like the animals they hunted, American Indians
knew better than to travel during blizzards. But what if
they were caught in an unexpected blizzard?

Willy Whitefeather tells his audiences about a
lifesaving method his ancestors used. First, they dug a
U-shaped tunnel in a snowbank, with a place to sit at
the curve of the U. This shape blocked the wind. The
Indians carried a long stick into the tunnel and
blocked the entrance behind them with snow so the

wind wouldn't enter it. They then poked an air hole through the top of the snow with their stick, and sat in the "snow cave" until the blizzard stopped or rescuers came. A piece of colorful material tied to the stick helped others to find them.

Medicinal Plants

The American Indians had no drugstores and hospitals, yet medicine men and women possessed great knowledge of the healing value of many plants. Even the average Indian man and woman knew much about "natural" cures.

Here are a few of the plants the Indians counted on for their survival when they had medical problems:

Pennyroyal was used in the Eastern Woodlands as an insect repellent. In the Southwest, Indians rubbed onions on the skin for the same purpose. Meanwhile, some people in the southeastern United States smeared on the crushed roots of goldenseal mixed with animal fat to keep insects away.

Cuts and sores were often treated with various parts of evergreen trees. These included the pitch, inner bark, and needles of such trees as the balsam fir, pine, cedar, juniper, and spruce.

Poultices, which are soft, moist bandages, were used for various wounds. These were made from many sources, including the leaves of skunk cabbage, the inner bark of slippery elm, and the crushed roots of the cattail.

The Hopi Indians in the Southwest made a salve for burns by mixing the crushed roots of the cattail with fat. Eastern tribes used the pitch or boiled inner bark of balsam fir for the same purpose.

SURVIVAL TODAY

Although modern people may have matches to replace fire sets, and store-bought canteens to replace birch-bark containers, some things have not changed from the time the wilderness was home to the North American Indians.

Now, as then, we must keep our wits about us in unfamiliar situations. At such times, our lives can depend upon our ability to use the raw materials around us for food, shelter, tools, clothing, and more.

Knowledge of the earth is passed from one generation to the next.

In today's world, Indians and non-Indians alike are gaining new respect for the way that Indians think about their environment. By combining this respect with common sense you allow Mother Earth to help you and those you love to survive.

GLOSSARY

Awl. A punching tool often made from buffalo bone.

Bearpaw. The simplest form of snowshoe.

Bow-drill. A fire-making set used primarily in western North America.

Cherokee. A North American Indian tribe from the Southeast.

Cordage. Fastening material made from both animal and plant sources.

Deadfall. A kind of trap that makes use of a heavy stone or piece of wood falling on an animal.

Flake. A small, sharp stone tool made from a larger stone.

Flesher. A tool used for scraping fat and tissue from animal hide.

Fletching. Feathers on an arrow.

Jerky. Dried meat.

Moccasin. The most popular North American Indian footwear.

Navajo. A North American Indian tribe from the Southwest.

Ojibwa. (Chippewa) A North American Indian tribe from the Great Lakes region.

Paiute. A North American Indian tribe of the Great Basin.

Pemmican. A food often taken on trips by Indians, made from dried meat, berries, and animal fat.

Pitch. A kind of glue that comes from trees.

Quiver. A case for carrying arrows, often made from animal skin.

Rawhide. Untanned animal skin.

Sinew. The long, white fiber that joins muscle to bone in animals. Used as a fastener.

Snare. A kind of trap comprised of a noose and fastener.

Tipi. A portable shelter built by the Plains Indians from poles, animal skin, and sinew.

Travois. A form of transportation made from wood and cordage.

Wikiup. A simple form of shelter.

FOR FURTHER READING

Goodchild, Peter. *Survival Skills of the North American Indians*. Chicago: Chicago Review Press, 1984.

Hofsinde, Robert (Gray-Wolf). *Indian Fishing and Camping*. New York: William Morrow, 1963.

Hofsinde, Robert (Gray-Wolf). *Indian Hunting*. New York: William Morrow, 1962.

Levinson, David, and David Sherwood. *The Tribal Living Book*. Denver: Johnson Books, 1984.

Whitefeather, Willy. *Willy Whitefeather's Outdoor Survival Handbook for Kids*. Tucson: Harbinger House, 1990.

█NDEX